Opposites

Hard and Soft

Siân Smith

Raintree is an imprint of Capstone Global Library
Limited, a company incorporated in England and
Wales having its registered office at 7 Pilgrim Street,
London, EC4V 6LB – Registered company number:
6695582

www.raintreepublishers.co.uk
myorders@raintreepublishers.co.uk

Text © Capstone Global Library Limited 2015
First published in hardback in 2014
The moral rights of the proprietor have been
asserted.

Edited by Siân Smith, Diyan Leake, and Brynn Baker
Designed by Tim Bond and Peggie Carley
Picture research by Liz Alexander
Production by Victoria Fitzgerald
Originated by Capstone Global Library Ltd
Printed and bound in China

ISBN 978 1 406 28301 3
18 17 16 15 14
10 9 8 7 6 5 4 3 2 1

British Library Cataloguing in Publication Data
A full catalogue record for this book is available from
the British Library.

Acknowledgements
We would like to thank the following for permission to
reproduce photographs: Alamy: Design Pics Inc., 16;
Getty Images: Daniel Grill, 7, Jose Luis Pelaez Inc, 6,
Michael Wildsmith, 4, Tamara Murray, 9, 22b; Shutterstock:
aperturesound, 21 left, Brian A Jackson, 14, 22a,
cristovao, front cover left, f9photos, 13, Gordan, front
cover right, JI de Wetre-research, 12, JIANG HONGYAN,
8, 21 right, back cover top, Madlen, 20 left, Mariusz
Szczygiel, 18, mexrix, 5, back cover bottom, Pavel Ignatov,
20 right, roroto12p, 11, SoulCurry, 10

Every effort has been made to contact copyright holders
of material reproduced in this book. Any omissions will
be rectified in subsequent printings if notice is given to
the publisher.

Contents

Hard and soft

A brick is **hard**.

A feather is **soft**.

The bat is hard.

The pillow is soft.

The hammer is hard.

The play dough is soft.

A fork is hard.

A sponge is soft.

The shell is hard.

The sand is soft.

Is this ball hard or soft?

The
ball is
hard.

Is this bubble hard or soft?

The
bubble
is soft.

Is this hat hard or soft?

The hat is hard.

Hard and soft quiz

Which of these things are hard?

Which of these things are soft?

Answers on page 22

Picture glossary

hard solid and firm

soft easily pressed or bent into a different shape

Index

Answers to questions on pages 20 and 21

The bolts are hard.
The blanket is soft.

Notes for teachers and parents

BEFORE READING

Building background:

Show the children a book and some play dough. Ask them to feel them. Can they squish the book? Can they squish the dough? Explain that the book is hard and the play dough is soft.

AFTER READING

Recall and reflection:

What things in the book are hard (a brick, a bat, a fork, a hammer, a shell)? What things are soft (a feather, a pillow, play dough, a sponge)? What can you do to something that is soft that you can't do to something that is hard?

Sentence knowledge:

Help children to find pages with questions. How do they know?

Word knowledge (phonics):

Encourage children to point at the word *hard* on any page. Sound out the three phonemes in the word *h/ar/d*. Ask children to sound out each phoneme as they point at the letters and then blend the sounds together to make the word *hard*. Challenge them to think of words that rhyme with *hard* (card, guard, lard, yard).

Word recognition:

Ask children to point at the word *ball* on page 14 or 15.

AFTER-READING ACTIVITIES

Make up some riddles for children to guess what you've got hidden in your bag. It is thin. It is long. You use it to write. What is it? Then ask children if it is hard or soft. Do the same with a tissue. It is thin. It is light. You use it to blow your nose. What is it? Is a tissue hard or soft?

In this book

Topic

hard and soft

Sentence stems

1. This___ is ___.
2. The ___ is ___ .
3. A ___ is ___.
4. Is this ___ ___ or ___?

High-frequency words

a
and
are
is
of
or
the
these
this
which